TABLE OF CONTENTS

RESUPPLY AT THE BATTLE OF DIEN BIEN PHU: WHAT LESSONS WERE LEARNED AND HOW ARE THEY APPLIED IN TODAY'S MILITARY OPERATIONS

Army Transformation is leading the United States Army toward operations characterized by small separated unit operations with great strategic significance without the benefit of secure ground lines of communication linked to secure support bases. This implies that airlift and aerial resupply will play a major role in the deployment and sustainment of our forces during such operations and will determine the success of Army Transformation. While this is not a new concept, it does require unique considerations and capabilities in order to insure success. Historical evidence supports this claim, and no two battles prove this more than the battles of Dien Bien Phu and Khe Sanh. Much like the circumstances anticipated for the army of the future, comparisons reveal these two battles had strategic implications, were conducted in isolated locations at a significant distance from their supply bases, and were highly dependent on the aerial delivery of supplies for the successful outcome of the operation.[1] In the case of Khe Sanh the result was success, while Dien Bien Phu resulted in failure that brought with it devastating military and political consequences.[2]

The purpose of this paper is to examine the strategic significance of Dien Bien Phu and Khe Sanh and the impact logistics support had on the outcome of these operations. The further analysis of their contrasting differences, the lessons learned from these two operations and the current status of United States aerial resupply operations provide the reader with a better understanding of their significance in relationship to Army Transformation.

BACKGROUND

Dien Bien Phu and Khe Sanh were key events around which larger national goals and strategies pivoted. In each case the decision was made to force a fight to demonstrate national resolve and military dominance in order to force the Vietminh into negotiations. In the case of Dien Bien Phu the French were defeated because they did not commit enough resources to overcome a flawed strategy and gross operational miscalculations. After their defeat, the French Government lacked the will to continue the war and political leverage to avoid a hastened settlement with the Vietminh. Their ultimate surrender of northern Indochina contributed to the downfall of the Cabinet of Premier Laniel and reversed more than a century of empire building.[3]

The same political and operational concerns were raised 14 years later during the planning phase of Khe Sanh. With the political ramifications of Dien Bien Phu prevalent in

President Johnson's mind he was fully aware of Khe Sanh's potential impact on his political future and his war policy as a whole. There was little doubt that should the Vietminh overrun Khe Sanh, a major psychological blow would be struck against the Administration's war policy.[4]

Once again a tactical battle was intended to display a nation's determination and commitment to the war effort that only a successful military operation could provide. The difference at Khe Sanh was the Americans developed a plan that was within their capability to support and execute while the French did not. Ultimately the desired outcome was to convince the communists to seek negotiations for an honorable peace rather than continue their aggression as a means to affect political change. With Khe Sanh as a display of commitment, President Johnson left his options open by declaring the United States remained ready "to send its representatives to any forum, at any time, to discuss the means of bringing this ugly war to an end."[5]

Within a relatively short span of time, two tactical battles occurred in the same location of the world, against the same enemy, upon which a nation's strategy for the conduct of the war hinged. The success or failure of the operation came down to the ability to aerial resupply an isolated force located some distance from its support base. One operation ended in success. The other resulted in failure.

DIEN BIEN PHU

Influencing French commitment and strategic policy in Indochina was the war's unpopularity in France. Because of this, the government did not draft Frenchmen to serve or fight in Indochina.[6] The lack of public support also contributed to political instability and a lack of will to continue the war. Even with these considerations Vietnam remained the centerpiece of French commitment to contain communism because of China's potential to influence French economic development in the region.

The situation in France made the tactical commander's efforts to conduct the war difficult. The lack of support for the war in France equated to a lack of resources committed to the war effort. When the war began, French forces held huge advantages over the Vietnamese in terms of manpower, weapons, transport, and military organization. This began to change. The Vietminh were fighting in their own country for their own liberation and livelihood. This was quickly becoming an important factor in the increase of Vietnamese commitment to the war.

This commitment was a challenge for the newly appointed French commander. The French government instructed him to take a fresh look at the military situation in Indochina and correct the mistakes that previous commanders had made. However, they also made it clear they did not expect him to win the war but merely prevent the military situation from getting worse while they attempted to arrange a cease-fire with the Vietnamese. With this guidance the French commander developed a plan for the operation at Dien Bien Phu. With the intention of restoring the confidence of his troops, shifting the French war effort out of neutral through offensive action, and placing France in a position to negotiate for peace by reversing French fortunes in the region, the plan to defend Dien Bien Phu was implemented.

Unfortunately the plan was doomed to failure. Arguably there were several factors that contributed to the failures at Dien Bien Phu but none more prominent then the implementation of an aggressive operation without consideration for the resources required to support it. To conduct their operation the French chose a location in a valley near the village of Dien Bien Phu, 200 miles by air from their main supply base in Hanoi. The only road linking Dien Bien Phu with Hanoi was Route 41, which twisted and turned over the mountains making the road distance 300 miles between the two points. The Vietminh controlled the road, which prevented the French from transporting men or equipment on it. From the very beginning of the battle the only way to access and resupply the isolated base was by air.[7] This situation created an immediate problem because of the volume of supplies required to support the garrison and the physical limitations on delivering them. The scenario was clear. It involved small separated unit operations with great strategic significance without the benefit of secure ground lines of communication linked to secure support bases.

Initially the support mission went well with airdrops consisting of every category of supply imaginable. Included in these drops was ammunition, electric generators, empty sandbags, gasoline stoves, cases of wine, beer and pastries.[8] Over the next 167 days of the siege a total of 10,400 air missions were flown in support of Dien Bien Phu of which 6,700 were supply or troop-transport missions.[9]

While the logistic challenges were numerous four areas stand out as the major contributors to placing a strain on lift capacity. These include the availability of aircraft, the amount and type of supplies required to sustain the base, the denial by the enemy of the use of the runway for air landings, and the inability to recover air dropped supplies. It quickly became apparent the availability of aircraft was a problem. The transport force consisted of 100 C-47s and 20 C119s. Additional available assets included the American Central Intelligence Agency's Air America and a mixed bag of civilian aircraft that included Bristol Freighters, a 307B Stratoliner, C-46s, and DC-4s.[10] The size of the fleet coupled with an undermanned maintenance force prevented the French from ever having more than 100 supply aircraft available on any one given day.[11] To maintain combat effectiveness the base required a minimum of 200 tons of supplies per day but throughout the operation the aerial resupply effort only averaged 123 tons per day. Factoring in the amount of supplies that were damaged, the delivery of usable supplies reduced this figure to 100 tons per day.[12]

The volume of supplies required by the base placed a strain on the logistics system even before the fighting began. The delivery of a light squadron of M-24 "General Chaffee" tanks was an early indication of logistical challenges. After being dismantled, a single tank required a total of seven aircraft to transport it to the garrison. Most of the tank was loaded on five C-47's, but the tank hull weighing four tons required two British Bristol freight aircraft with frontal clamshell doors to accommodate its loading and off loading. Upon arrival the mechanics began the assembly process which required two days to assemble a single tank.[13]

Other logistical challenges included supplying the garrison with food due to the cultural diversity of the French garrison. At a minimum, six different types of food rations were allocated to accommodate the European, North African, African, Vietnamese, T'ai Auxiliary, and "PIM"-PW's soldiers occupying Dien Bien Phu.[14] The standard meat of American or French canned rations were unacceptable to the pork-shunning Moslems and the Europeans could not subsist on rice. Health risks also were also a consideration. A concerted effort to deliver healthy food was also attempted to prevent disease. The longer a soldier remained in the garrison the more susceptible he was of falling victim to disease connected with the lack of vitamins. To prevent this, a priority effort was made to supply the men with raw onions and fruits even during the worst periods of the battle.[15]

A list of major consumable supply items delivered to Dien Bien Phu shows the peculiarly "French" aspects of the problem.

Rice	791 tons
Frozen meat	195 tons
Dried bread	473 tons
Fresh vegetables	25 tons
Individual combat rations	623,194
Survival rations	22,760
Wine	49,720 gallons
Wine concentrate	7,062 gallons
Mustard	60 kilograms

The logistical constraints of the operation continued to take on a life of their own. Of all the supply commodities the requirements for construction material was insurmountable. The standard of fortifying a position to resist artillery shells of 105-mm was known before the operation began but the amount of construction material required to achieve this standard was ignored. The quantity of construction material to adequately fortify the base was 36,000 tons.[16] The overburdened supply system only provided 3,300 tons. Based on the materials available priority was given to fortifying the underground rooms used by the base commander, the radio operators, and the X-ray specialists of the hospital.[17]

In an attempt to supplement their supply of construction material the French gathered materials from the surrounding area. They began by taking apart every building and shed in the surrounding villages but found transporting these materials back to the garrison was nearly impossible due to a lack of transport vehicles and the roadless jungle. In total the engineers collected around 2,200 tons of construction wood which left the garrison about 34,000 tons short of their minimal engineering requirements. In raw statistics this represented the cargo loads of about 12,000 C-47 transport aircraft. Various figures exist but around eighty aircraft were available on any one given day to make the flight to Dien Bien Phu. Assuming nothing else but engineering materials were flown into Dien Bien Phu, it would have taken five months to make the base a defensible field position.[18]

The limited effectiveness of the air fleet was reduced even further when the French lost complete use of their airstrip as a result of Vietminh artillery. For the remainder of the battle, supplies had to be air dropped into Dien Bien Phu. The base was ill equipped to conduct such a large supply recovery operation. As the Vietminh pushed closer to the fortifications, drop zones became smaller and any men and supplies dropped too soon or too late fell directly into enemy units. Those supplies that did find their way into the perimeter required a dangerous effort to retrieve and deliver them to the proper recipients. The lack of recovery assets made it impossible to move items like electric field generators weighing one ton, or single five-ton "palette" loads. These loads often remained where they landed. Other complications resulted when loads experiencing parachute failure plowing into entrenchment's with all the impact of a heavy bomb.

In the end, overwhelmed by the Vietminh and unable to overcome their logistical shortfalls the French surrendered Dien Bien Phu. The French lost the battle because they grossly underestimated the Vietminh capabilities, were unable to neutralize Vietminh artillery, overestimated their own air lift and logistical capability, and the limitations placed on the theater commander by the French Government.[19] These limitations undermined the aggressive military action undertaken to support the French strategy of bolstering their military position in an attempt to force the Vietminh into negotiations for a peaceful settlement of the war.

KHE SANH

The decision to defend the base at Khe Sanh was in response to the Vietminh's strategy for conducting the war. During the first Indochina War the Lao Dong Party had brilliantly coordinated a military and diplomatic strategy to convince the French it would be madness to continue their struggle. The North Vietnamese leaders in 1966 believed it was necessary to move into a similar phase of simultaneous negotiating and fighting.[20] According to their timetable the war was currently in the fighting stage, in which they believed the Americans had an advantage. The next phase was the fighting-while-negotiating stage. During this phase the objective was to conduct military operations in a manner which would increase the governments negotiating position. In this phase the Communists felt they would have the advantage over the Americans, who were unskilled at diplomatic and political warfare. In July 1967 Resolution 13 was issued from Hanoi officially adopting this strategy.[21] The fighting-and-negotiating phase of the war began. Aware of this strategy, the Americans believed the Communists would attempt to achieve a major victory in the Quang Tri and Thua Thien provinces and then seek negotiations.[22]

Ironically the American strategy was very similar. The goal of the United States was to negotiate an honorable peace that would enable the nations of Southeast Asia to concentrate on economic and social needs. To achieve this goal President Johnson believed conducting successful military operations would convince the Vietminh that peace was preferable to fighting. The President maintained that American success would serve as "a concrete demonstration that aggression across international frontiers or demarcation lines was no longer an acceptable means of political change."[23] Although the strategy of the Americans and the French 14 years earlier are almost identical the outcome at Khe Sanh was completely different. Affecting the success was the distance to supply bases, availability of aircraft, and logistical support capability.

Khe Sanh was chosen as part of this larger strategy because of its location in the Quang Tri province in the northwest corner of South Vietnam. The base sat atop a plateau in the shadow of the Dong Tri Mountain and overlooked a tributary of the Quang Tri river.[24] Its location of just over 100 miles from the supply base at Da Nang made it a supportable defensive strongpoint, to canalize Communist movements and to support American operations against infiltration routes entering South Vietnam.[25]

During the planning phase of the operation the decision to defend Khe Sanh took into account the re-supply distance from the supply base at Da Nang. As a result at no time during the operation did mission requirements exceed the support systems capability to support the garrison. To accomplish this, an orchestrated centralized effort insured the continuous flow of supplies into Khe Sanh. When possible, aircraft were co-located with the supply base at Da Nang. Other air missions originating from bases at Tan Son Nhut, Cam Rahn Bay, and Tuy Hoa, stopped at Da Nang to load supplies prior to flying to Khe Sanh.[26] Maintenance personnel and mission coordinators stationed at Da Nang provided critical support before the final flight to Khe Sanh. After the last maintenance point at Da Nang the flight time to Khe Sanh was only half an hour.[27]

In support of this operation were 2,000 U.S. aircraft available in Southeast Asia.[28] The primary aircraft used were the C-130, C-123, and C-7A. These aircraft reflected advancements in technology over the past 14 years. From a pure tonnage perspective the most efficient of the Air Force transports was the C-130, with a maximum payload in excess of 20 tons, enabling it to deliver an average of 13 tons per sortie during the battle. Tonnage was not its only attribute. The C-130 had a rapid airborne offload system, which could deposit four pallets of cargo on the ramp within 30 seconds. The Fairchild C-123 was capable of carrying 8 tons of cargo and the de Haviland C-7A was built to deliver 3 tons of cargo.[29] These assets ensured an uninterrupted flow of supplies.

The Americans also enjoyed a marked superiority in logistical support.[30] Unlike the French, at no time during the operation at Khe Sanh did the base's basic stocks of food, fuel, or ammunition near depletion.[31] This is attributed to sound planning. It was determined that the upper limit that can be effectively sustained in a protracted situation where only one runway is available is around 10,000 men.[32] For this reason there were never more then 7,000 men garrisoned at Khe Sanh at any one time. As a result, the American support requirements never exceeded its capability. The estimated supply requirement to sustain Khe Sanh was 235 tons per day.[33] While the tonnage delivered to Khe Sanh varied throughout the operation depending on the tactical situation, the lowest average for any period was 250 tons and the highest average was 350 tons of supplies a day.[34] All these figures exceeded the daily supply requirement.

The base itself contained an efficient logistical support capability. On the ground at Khe Sanh was an Air Force contingent as well as personnel from the 109th QM Company that controlled airlift operations, made emergency repairs to aircraft, organized recovery operations, and assisted in cargo handling.[35] The garrison also had immediate access to a host of other logistics specialists located throughout the theater. These resources proved invaluable. Because of the effectiveness of the resupply effort, the military determined that Khe Sanh was not a siege like Dien Bien Phu but a battle in which the Marines were at the most forward salient in the front lines.[36] Compared to the French, it is clear the Americans had a better grasp of logistics and a more robust capability which translated into mission success.

The magnitude of the Khe Sanh resupply operation was staggering. As already mentioned Khe Sanh required 235 tons of supplies per day to sustain operations.[37] The total number of aerial resupply missions flown was 9,109 sorties, transporting 14,562 passengers, and delivering 17,091 tons of cargo to Khe Sanh.[38] The airdrop mission exceeded the total for all of Vietnam before that time. Airdrop accounted for an additional 8,120 tons of cargo parachuted to the defenders in 601 individual sorties.[39] Comparisons of Dien Bien Phu and Khe Sanh in cold statistical data suggests an analysis of logistical requirements is essential in determining a successful operation.

	Dien Bien Phu	Khe Sanh
Distance from friendly support bases	100 miles plus	100 miles (Da Nang)
Airfield status	Unusable	Usable (for C123s)
"External" artillery support	None	175mm guns (Rock Pile, Camp Carroll)
Available daily tactical combat aircraft	100	1,500
Average incoming rounds (daily)	2,000 plus	150
Aircraft losses	62	7
Aerial resupply (daily)	100 tons	161 tons plus
How replacements arrived	Parachute	Helicopters and fixed wing aircraft
Evacuation of wounded	None	Helicopter
Enemy efforts after first ground Action	Continuous	Four assaults though March, then probes
Average air combat sorties (daily)	22	300
Average heavy bomber sorties (daily)	None	45-50

Passengers air-landed/evacuated via   0/0   2,676/1,574
Cargo aircraft

President Johnson hailed Khe Sanh as a decisive victory citing the Vietminh failure to achieve a major victory in the Quang Tri and Thua Thien provinces.[40] Fundamental to this victory was the United States planning and execution of an operation that was logistically supportable. The United States drew upon its marked logistical superiority to succeed in an operation against an enemy strikingly similar to the situation encountered by the French, which resulted in failure. Several factors contributed to the operational success. First, was the operational planners' understanding of the critical relationship of distance to support bases which reduced the potential strain on airlift. Second was the centralized control of aerial supply operations, which took full advantage of available resources, contributed to a coordinated operation, and reduced the duplication of effort during the resupply process. Finally, the determination to garrison an appropriate number of soldiers at Khe Sanh that could accomplish the mission and be adequately supported resulted in the garrisons supply requirements never exceeding the logistics systems capability to support them.

CURRENT STATUS OF U.S. AERIAL RESUPPLY

As the mission at Khe Sanh demonstrates aerial resupply has been an integral part of military operations for many years. In fact airdrop missions have supported actions in every major conflict or operation the U.S. Army has participated in from WWII to today. Advancements in technology have profoundly improved the Army's ability to resupply its forces with increased efficiency. These improvements include aircraft capability, delivery techniques and procedures which all contribute to making aerial resupply a force multiplier.[41]

Specific improvements include the C17 aircraft, A22 Container Delivery System (CDS), timer activated canopy releases, the Tri-walled Aerial Delivery System (TRIADS), the Low Cost Aerial Delivery System (LCADS) , the Enhanced container Delivery System (ECDS), and the Humanitarian Airdrop Container System (HACS).[42] LCADS features a prepackaged, one –time use parachute, which can be used at all altitudes. The greatest advantage of LCADS is its impact on efficiency as its production cost is about one half of the current 26-foot ring slot parachute in use today. A second advantage is having the parachute prepackaged at the manufacturer greatly decreases the time required to rig supplies, which reduces Army rigger's workload. As a result riggers can focus on the load itself instead of the time consuming process of packing or repairing parachutes.[43] ECDS improves the existing CDS. It uses a 463L-based platform that is easier to transport and rig. Using this method increases potential capacity from

9

the current 2,200 pounds to 10,000 pounds, increases accuracy at multiple altitudes, and reduces the amount of bundles required.[44] The HACS designed for one-time use, consists of cardboard and durable plastic for the top and bottom. With recent military participation in a variety of operations this system was developed to reduce the cost of humanitarian relief operations. By receiving containers directly from the depot prepackaged and ready for airdrop the cost is about one-third of the current CDS system. Once received, riggers simply attach a skid board and disposable prepacked parachute and the container is ready for airdrop.[45]

As the names of some of these new systems indicate, current operations do not always involve the resupply of Army forces or the delivery of standard military supplies. In Bosnia, airdrop was used as a method of delivering humanitarian relief. Provide Promise is the largest humanitarian airdrop in U.S. History to date with the delivery of more than 30,000 bundles of humanitarian supplies. Deliveries included food, medical supplies and winterization items such as blankets, clothes, plastic sheeting, nails, candles and tape.[46] During this operation primarily two types of airdrops were utilized. The first and largest number was high velocity airdrops from altitudes of 10,000 to 18,000 feet using the (CDS) in over 200 different configurations to deliver food and medical supplies during the operation.[47] The CDS bundles were dropped using an A-22 cargo bag and five layers of honeycomb mounted on ¾ inch plywood. To soften the impact a 26 foot ring slot parachute was attached to the load reducing its speed to 55 miles per hour at point of impact. When the proper amount of padding was used even the most fragile medical supplies dropped without damage.[48]

The other airdrop method was free drop. When it was discovered that delivering a single package by airdrop attracted a large crowd in one location preventing food from being distributed evenly among the intended recipients, the situation was remedied by using the Tri-wall aerial Delivery System (TRIADS). This system consists of a cardboard Triwall box filled with 40 cases of individual Meals Ready to Eat (MREs). Once the boxes are ejected over the drop zone, webbing, holding the box together is yanked free by a static line. The precut boxes break open scattering 480 MREs over a wide area, decreasing the chance of injury to people waiting on the ground.[49]

During Provide Comfort the 5th Quartermaster Detachment rigged over 7,600 CDS bundles and packed over 6,7000 parachutes.[50] The methods used in this operation mirrored Operation Provide Promise with the high velocity delivery method used in 76% of total airdrops, and the low velocity method used in 24% of them.[51]

Even in less lengthy operations, such as Just Cause, C-130 and C-141 aircraft airdropped over 683 tons of equipment and supplies.[52] During the Persian Gulf War aerial resupply was used to support the XVIII Airborne Corps. Air Force intratheater air assets moved thousands of soldiers, tons of rolling stock, and vital repair parts in support of the Corps preparation for offensive operations. During their displacement from defensive positions to offensive tactical assembly areas, 2,703 wheeled vehicles, 15,848 passengers, and 116 pallets were moved into place in just 14 days.[53] In addition, they received aerial bulk fuel delivery service, which provided the Corps with significant operational flexibility. Each day aircraft delivered 100,000 to 120,000 gallons of fuel to Log Base Charlie, using a field landing strip constructed from a two-lane paved road by Army engineers.[54] This capability was enough to sustain operational requirements of the 101st Airborne Division. If required the air resupply operation was prepared to shift forward into Iraq had the war lasted longer.[55]

IMPLICATIONS FOR TRANSFORMATION

For half a century, the U.S. Army has been organized and equipped to meet America's security needs for the Cold War.[56] This structure must change in order to remain a viable force ready to meet the needs of the Nation in the future. As the United States continues to move toward a CONUS-based force projection Army, aerial resupply is destined to play a vital role in the success of Army Transformation both at the strategic and tactical levels. This point becomes evident as the future army faces the possibility of conducting operations in regions lacking American military infrastructure. Under these conditions it is logical to anticipate an increase in military operations with strategic implications, conducted in isolated locations, separated by unsecured lines of communication, at great distances from their supply bases. To insure success and support the effort to reduce the logistical footprint in theater, strategic and tactical airlift will require close orchestration to ensure maximum use of throughput capacity.

Army Transformation is based on the Army Vision of being able to deploy, anywhere in the world, a brigade within four days, a division in five days, and five divisions within 30 days.[57] Included in this vision are seven broad goals designed to make the Army more responsive, deployable, agile, versatile, lethal, survivable, and sustainable.[58]

The initial force structure solution is the Interim Brigade Combat Team (IBCT). The IBCT's are being organized and equipped to deploy nearly as quickly as light infantry units, with more firepower and armored mobility for their soldiers. Designed to be lighter than the heavy brigade, the IBCT's will operate for three days with only their basic load of supplies and fuel. Additionally the heavy brigade's current requirement of 38 percent of its task organization being dedicated to support is reduced to only 19 percent an IBCT.[59] Coupled with their new equipment this is expected to reduce their airlift requirement to half that of a standard heavy brigade. In pure statistics by using the C-17 transport for baseline comparison, a heavy brigade requires approximately 430 C-17 sorties to deploy, while an IBCT will require approximately 212 C-17 sorties.[60]

Organization is not the only change to facilitate Army Transformation. Future Combat System (FCS) development criteria will require each vehicle to fit on a C-130 transport.[61] Compared to the current Abrams tanks, the future combat system will be 70 percent lighter and 50 percent smaller while maintaining equivalent lethality and survivability.[62] Based on current trends in military operations the Army will need a small but potent crisis force that can deploy from the continental United States and fight to retain freedom of maneuver. A strategic response force will follow behind it, if necessary, with the ability to enter the theater fighting and become a campaign winning force. The ultimate goal is to create a fighting corps that can deploy and fight within days. This ability will be the difference between a short, relatively bloodless campaign and a drawn-out war characterized by massive carnage. [63]

All of these goals and objectives are designed to create a force that can conduct operations closely resembling Dien Bien Phu and Khe Sanh but on a larger scale and over greater distances. Although the comparisons are striking, it must be pointed out that Army Transformation is not a result of the operations at Dien Bien Phu and Khe Sanh but rather the significance of the lessons learned from these operations will contribute to the success of Army Transformation. By design future organizations will deploy into tactical positions directly from the continental United States.[64] To accomplish this and simultaneously reduce the requirement for airlift the Army must reduce its logistics consumption during early phases of the campaign. The premise for this concept, is every load of logistics saved equates to more fighting organizations delivered in a shorter amount of time. It also means that forces will operate at greater distances from their support bases requiring an effective aerial resupply system.

Military leaders understand in order to accomplish this, current levels of available airlift must increase substantially.[65] In future operations the distance factors from support bases in CONUS to tactical units in theater will require strategic lift to deliver supply's along lines of communication covering thousands of miles. Once in theater the orchestration of strategic and tactical lift must be accomplished to support units conducting nonlinear operations in greater depth with wider dispersal to avoid being destroyed by precision weapons.[66] Along with airlift, ultimate success will depend upon combat service support's ability to support operations on a dispersed battlespace.[67] Discontinuous logistical operations will be the norm because it will not be practical to maintain open and secure lines of communication to forward tactical organizations on a continuous basis.[68] For this reason organizational design and battle rhythms must accommodate the need for periodic logistical and recuperative activities.[69] Mountains of Iron will no longer apply. Logistical operations will have to be so effective that organizations will have just enough redundancy to absorb losses or enough to defend themselves if temporarily isolated. With this view of the future force the logistician must understand the aspects of the tactical situation, anticipate requirements and provide support to multiple isolated areas over great distances. While this is a challenge for logisticians, it is achievable through appropriate levels of available transport aircraft and the efficient use of strategic and tactical airlift.

CONCLUSION

The concepts addressed by Army Transformation are achievable as long as the Army's support structure transitions from a Cold War structure to one that is more responsive, deployable, agile, versatile, and survivable. The basic premise logisticians must understand is Army Transformation is leading the Army toward operations characterized by small separated unit operations with great strategic significance conducted without the benefit of secure ground lines of communication linking forces to secure support bases. The support operations involved in aerial resupply will be critical in these operations. As is evident by the operations discussed in this paper, logisticians have been supporting these types of operations for over 50 years. The doctrinal foundation for aerial resupply is sound and has been effectively implemented in recent years. Army Transformation does not require the reinvention of techniques, practices or procedures. Army Transformation is merely requiring aerial resupply operations be conducted on a grander scale over greater distances.

The basic concepts remain the same. The risks associated with independent type aerial resupply operations is known. Almost without exception all isolated operations of any significance have been conducted against an overwhelming enemy buildup potential. It is evident that the successful operations have denied the enemy the opportunity of exercising their superior buildup potential, given an adequate amount of airlift to support the mission and access to an adequate number of airfields.[70] This has been accomplished by the early entry of forces into the region, coupled with an early link-up with follow on forces. In Army Transformation this is the role of the strategic response force.

To accomplish this, aerial resupply and airlift will be critical in deploying adequate forces to the region and supporting them during the operation. Reducing the logistical footprint in theater to accommodate the deployment of more combat forces means support bases will be located at great distances from supported units. No longer can strategic lift move supplies from CONUS to large support bases in theater with tactical lift moving the same supplies forward. To maximize throughput capacity of aircraft, CONUS support bases will be required to build support packages tailored to meet specific unit/operational needs and deliver them directly to unit locations in theater. This reduction in transloading operations reduces the requirement for logistical support and reduces the amount of aircraft involved in the movement of supplies. The use of tactical lift will continue on a smaller scale providing flexibility by transporting emergency resupplys and addressing specific unit needs. As this paper reveals, the concept of the U.S. Air Force providing key aerial resupply to isolated locations is not a new one. Advancements in aircraft, delivery systems, and technology used in operations like Tuzla and Mogadishu display the effectiveness of aerial resupply but these operations were limited in size. In order to address the increased needs of Army Transformation more airlift may be required. According to former Air Force Secretary F. Whitten Peters, "expeditionary operations, as planned by the Air Force and now as planned by our sister services, are going to require more strategic airlift."[71] This claim is supported by others who indicate the USAF strategic fleet is inadequate to support the stated national strategy of being able to conduct two widely separated major theater wars fought in close succession.[72] This claim is substantiated. The General Accounting Office, in a study of airlift capabilities found that the Air Force is short about a third of the organic airlift necessary to meet our national strategy requirements.[73] In the final analysis it comes down to a matter of supply and demand. The ratio of aircraft needed is in direct relationship to the amount and type required to be moved. These requirements may vary due to political considerations, weapons involved, or geographic region but based on past operations success comes down to a simple formula. The amount of aircraft required depends on the number of troops to be supported, tonnage to be delivered, airlift distances to be flown, supply capabilities of support bases, duration of airlift effort, and the ability to support airlift operations in the theater of operations. When these considerations are addressed historical evidence reveals that aerial resupply operations are successful.

WORD COUNT = 6375

ENDNOTES

[1] Howard R. Simpson, <u>Dien Bien Phu: The Epic Battle America Forgot</u> (Washington, London: Brassey's, Inc., 1994), 62.

[2] Dr. David K. Vaughan, <u>From Stalingrad to Khe Sanh: Factors in the Successful Use of Tactical Airlift to Support Isolated Land Battle Areas</u> (Washington D.C: U.S. Government Printing Office, 1969), 1.

[3] Ibid., 8.

[4] Peter Braestrap, <u>Big Story: How the American Press and Television Reported and Interpreted the Crises of Tet 1968 in Vietnam and Washington</u> (New Haven and London: Yale University Press, Alpine Press, 1977), 264.

[5] Bernard C. Nalty, <u>Air Power and The Fight For Khe Sanh</u> (Washington D.C., Office of Air Force History, 1973),106.

[6] Peter A. Poole, <u>Dien Bien Phu, 1954: The Battle That Ended the First Indochina War</u> (New York: Franklin Watts, Inc,1972), 30.

[7] Ibid., 31.

[8] Simpson, 66.

[9] Bernard B. Fall, <u>Hell In A Very Small Place: The Siege Of Dien Bien Phu</u> (Philadelphia, New York: J.B. Lippincott Company, 1966), 458.

[10] Walter J. Boyne, "Airpower at Khe Sanh," <u>Air Force Magazine</u> , August 1998, 6.

[11] Fall, 97.

[12] Vaughan, 3.

[13] Fall, 97.

[14] Ibid., 246.

[15] Ibid., 246.

[16] Poole, 32.

[17] Ibid., 33.

[18] Fall, 89.

[19] Norman E. Martin, "Dien Bien Phu And The Future Of Airborne Operations," <u>Military Review</u>, June 1956, 34.

[20] James I. Marino, "Strategic Crossroads at Khe Sanh,"; available from <http://www.thehistorynet.com/Vietnam/articles/1999/1299_text.htm>; Internet; accessed 23 January 2001, 3.

[21] Ibid., 4.

[22] Ibid., 8.

[23] Nalty, 22.

[24] Vaughan, 4.

[25] Nalty, 21.

[26] Boyne, 6.

[27] Nalty, 54.

[28] Vaughan, 19.

[29] Nalty, 20.

[30] Ibid., 19.

[31] Ibid., 7.

[32] Ibid., 7.

[33] Vaughan, 5.

[34] Marino, 9.

[35] Peter Brush, "Lifeline To Khe Sanh: The 109th Quartermaster Company (Air Delivery),"; available from <http://chss.montclair.edu/english/furr/Vietnam/pb109.html>; Internet; accessed 3 January 2001, 3.

[36] Marino, 9.

[37] Vaughan, 5.

[38] Ibid., 5.

[39] Nalty, 58.

[40] Ibid., 103.

[41] Martin, 26.

[42] "Air Drop / Aerial Delivery Development," available from <http://www. Quartermaster.army.mil/ltd/CLC3%20Papers/CLC3%20Pa.../heavyequipairdrop.htm>; Internet; accesed 3 Janurary 2001, 2.

[43] CPT Stephen R. Davis, "Emerging Technology In Airdrop Operations," available from <http://www.qmfound.com/air_bosnia.htm>; Internet; accessed 4 January 2001. 3.

[44] Ibid., 3.

[45] Ibid., 3.

[46] Ibid., 2.

[47] Ibid., 1.

[48] "Air Drop / Aerial Delivery Development," available from <http://www. Quartermaster.army.mil/ltd/CLC3%20Papers/CLC3%20Pa.../heavyequipairdrop.htm>; Internet; accesed 3 Janurary 2001, 11.

[49] Ibid., 2.

[50] Ibid., 10.

[51] Ibid., 11.

[52] Ibid., 10.

[53] LTC Christopher R. Paparone, "How Does The Gulf War Measure Up?,"; available from <http://www.gulflink.osd.mil/water_use/water_use_refs/n32en035/ms309.htm>; Internet; accessed 4 February 2001, 5.

[54] Ibid.

[55] Ibid.

[56] Dennis Steele, "A 30-Minute Course On The Army's 30 Year Overhaul," Army Magazine, February 2001, 22.

[57] John A. Tirpak, "A Clamor For Airlift," Air Force Magazine, December 2000, 3.

[58] Ibid., 23.

[59] Ibid., 34.

[60] Ibid., 34.

[61] Ibid., 32.

[62] BG Huba Wass de Czege (ret), "Six Compelling Ideas On The Road To A Future Army: Insights From The Army's Study Efforts Since Gen. Gordon R. Sullivan's Louisiana Maneuvers," <u>Army Magazine</u>, February 2001, 40.

[63] Ibid., 44.

[64] Ibid., 45.

[65] Ibid., 44.

[66] Ibid., 45.

[67] Ibid.

[68] Ibid.

[69] Ibid.

[70] Norman E. Martin, "<u>Dien Bien Phu And The Future Of Airborne Operations</u>," <u>Military Review</u>, June 1956, 25.

[71] Tirpak, 2.

[72] Ibid.

[73] Ibid., 3.

BIBLIOGRAPHY

Alexander, Paul. "Dien Bien Phu: One of Vietnam's proudest moments." January 2001. Available from <http://seattletimes.nwsource.com/news/nation_rld/htm198/altphoo_19990507.html>. Internet. Accessed 4 January 2001.

Born, K. "Quatermaster Aerial Delivery: The Story of the Airborne Rigger." January 2001. Available from <http://www.qmfound.com/rigger.htm>. Internet. Accessed 4 January 2001.

Braestrap, Peter. Big Story: How the American Press and Television Reported and Interpreted the Crises of Tet 1968 in Vietnam and Washington. New Haven, Yale University Press, 1977.

Boyne Walter J., "Airpower at Khe Sanh." Air Force Magazine, August 1998, 3-12.

Brush Peter. "Lifeline To Khe Sanh: The 109th Quartermaster Company (Air Delivery)."September 1996. Available from <http://chss.montclair.edu/english/furr/Vietnam/pb109.html>. Internet. Accessed 3 January 2001

Bundy, McGeorge. "France in Vietman, 1954, and the U.S. in Vietnam." June 1965. Available from http://ww.uwm.edu/People.mbradley/mcgeorgedoc2.html>. Internet. Accessed 3 January 2001.

Davis, Stephen R. "Emerging Technology In Airdrop Operations." Autumn 1997. Available from <http://www.qmfound.com/air_bosnia.htm> .Internet. Accessed 3 January 2001.

Fall, Bernard B. Hell In A Very Small Place: The Siege Of Dien Bien Phu. New York: J.B. Lippincott Company, 1966

Farmen, William N. "Ad Hoc Logistics in Bosnia." Joint Forces Quarterly (Autumn/Winter 1999-2000): 21-40.

Marino, James I. "Strategic Crossroads at Khe Sanh." December 1999. Available from <http://www.thehistorynet.com/Vietnam/articles/1999/1299_text.htm> .Internet. Accessed 4 January 2001.

Martin, Norman E. "Dien Bien Phu And The Future Of Airborne Operations." Military Review, June 1956, 30-46.

Nalty, Bernard C. Air Power and The Fight For Khe Sanh. Washington D.C: Office of Air Force History, 1973.

Paparone, Christopher R. "How Does The Gulf War Measure Up?" January 2001. Available from <http://www.gulflink.osd.mil/water_use/water_use_refs/n32en035/ms309.htm>. Internet. Accessed 4 January 2001.

Poole, Peter A. Dien Bien Phu, 1954: The Battle That Ended the First Indochina War. New York: Franklin Watts Inc, 1972.

Prados, John. <u>The Sky Would Fall Operation Vulture: The U.S. Bombing Mission In Indochina</u>. New York: The Dial Press, 1983.

Steele, Dennis. "The Army Magazine Hooah Guide to Army Transformation." <u>Army Magazine</u>, February 2001, 33-50.

Simpson, Howard R. <u>Dien Bien Phu: The Epic Battle America Forgot</u>. London: Brassey's, Inc., 1994.

Tirpak, John A. "A Clamor For Airlift." <u>Air Force Magazine</u>, December 2000, 16-27.

Vaughan, David K. Dr. <u>From Stalingrad to Khe Sanh: Factors in the Successful Use of Tactical Airlift to Support Isolated Land Battle Areas</u>. Washington D.C: U.S. Government Printing Office, 1969.

Wass de Czege, Huba. "Six Compelling Ideas On The Road To A Future Army: Insights From The Army's Study Efforts Since Gen. Gordon R. Sullivan's Louisiana Maneuvers." <u>Army Magazine</u>, February 2001, 15-36.